Landmark
Events in
American
History

# The Settling of
# Jamestown

Janet Riehecky

**WORLD ALMANAC® LIBRARY**

Please visit our web site at: www.worldalmanaclibrary.com
For a free color catalog describing World Almanac® Library's list of high-quality
books and multimedia programs, call 1-800-848-2928 (USA) or 1-800-387-3178
(Canada). World Almanac® Library's fax: (414) 332-3567.

Library of Congress Cataloging-in-Publication Data

Riehecky, Janet, 1953-
 The settling of Jamestown / by Janet Riehecky.
  p. cm. — (Landmark events in American history)
 Summary: Examines the founding of the English colony at Jamestown, its struggle
for survival, and its eventual decline.
 Includes bibliographical references and index.
 ISBN 0-8368-5341-5 (lib. bdg.)
 ISBN 0-8368-5355-5 (softcover)
 1. Jamestown (Va.)—History—17th century—Juvenile literature. 2. Pioneers—
Virginia—Jamestown—History—17th century—Juvenile literature. 3. Frontier and
pioneer life—Virginia—Jamestown—Juvenile literature. 4. Virginia—History—Colonial
period, ca. 1600-1775—Juvenile literature. [1. Jamestown (Va.)—History. 2. Virginia—
History—Colonial period, ca. 1600-1775.] I. Title. II. Series.
 F234.J3R53 2002
 975.5'425101—dc21
                               2002023451

This North American edition first published in 2002 by
**World Almanac® Library**
330 West Olive Street, Suite 100
Milwaukee, WI 53212 USA

This U.S. edition © 2002 by World Almanac® Library.

Produced by Discovery Books
Editor: Sabrina Crewe
Designer and page production: Sabine Beaupré
Photo researcher: Sabrina Crewe
Maps and diagrams: Stefan Chabluk
World Almanac® Library editorial direction: Mark J. Sachner
World Almanac® Library art direction: Tammy Gruenewald
World Almanac® Library production: Susan Ashley

Photo credits: Association for the Preservation of Virginia Antiquities: pp. 17 top, 25, 30,
42; Corbis: pp. 6, 8, 10, 26, 27; Granger Collection: pp. 9, 12, 24, 33, 39; Jamestown-
Yorktown Foundation: cover, pp. 4, 13, 43; Library of Congress: p. 37; National Park
Service, Colonial National Historical Park: pp. 15, 28, 31; North Wind Picture Archives:
pp. 5, 7, 11, 16, 17 bottom, 21, 22, 23, 29, 32, 35, 36, 38, 40, 41.

Printed in the United States of America

1 2 3 4 5 6 7 8 9 06 05 04 03 02

# Contents

# Introduction

In 1607, three ships landed on the coast of **Virginia**. The people on board had been sent by the Virginia Company of London, in England, to start a settlement in North America. The small and troubled settlement of Jamestown, built that year, was the beginning of the **colony** of Virginia. This was the first of what would become the British colonies in North America.

## The First British Colony

The Jamestown colonists hoped to find the same kind of wealth in North America that other Europeans had in colonies around the world. But reality differed greatly from the colonists' expectations. There was no gold, and many of the first colonists died from starvation and disease. The colonists were unwilling or unable to look after themselves, and there was conflict with some of the Native American people who were already living in the area. The arrival of supplies and new colonists from England, and the assistance of the Native population, barely kept the settlement from failing altogether.

## New Opportunities

The first of the settlers to arrive at Jamestown did not succeed in fulfilling their dreams, but they became part of something more significant. In sixteenth-century Europe, the wealth, power, and land belonged to a small ruling class. In an attempt to entice people to emigrate to North America, the Virginia Company offered new colonists opportunities they would never have had in England. In 1614, settlers in Virginia were granted a few acres of land to farm for themselves. It was a small step toward independence for poorer people.

## Self-government

The Virginia Company also decided it might help colonists' attitudes if they had some say in how they were governed. The establishment of the House of **Burgesses** in 1619 gave the Virginia colonists a chance to vote for local representatives to lead them. The House of Burgesses was the first **legislature** in the American colonies. Its limited powers and membership meant that it was a long way from true **democracy**, but it was a start.

As the colony of Virginia grew, the original settlement at Jamestown was eventually abandoned. Other towns attracted more settlers. But Jamestown will always be remembered for laying the foundation for representative government in America.

The settlement of Jamestown brought huge changes to the original inhabitants of Virginia, the Powhatan Indians. One of the most legendary Powhatans was Opechancanough, shown here being captured by colonist John Smith, one of the founders of Jamestown.

## Colonial Powers

During the 1500s, many nations, including France, the Netherlands, Portugal, Switzerland, Sweden, Germany, and Spain, sent explorers to the Americas. By the late 1500s, the powerful Spanish Empire controlled Mexico, Florida, and much of the Caribbean and South America. They enslaved Native people and carried back to Spain huge amounts of gold and silver. England hoped to gain similar riches from its colonies in North America.

# Virginia's Original Inhabitants

Before European settlers traveled to North America, many Native peoples lived there. The land that would become the colony of Virginia hosted about forty **Algonquian** groups. They lived in hundreds of villages scattered throughout the Virginia area. The languages, traditions, and lifestyles of these different Native groups were similar, yet distinct.

## Indian Dress and Decoration

This illustration of two Algonquian chiefs was based on drawings by English artist John White, who visited Virginia in the late 1500s and drew some of the first images of Native Americans to be seen in Europe.

Native dress was often more comfortable and practical than that worn by Europeans in the 1600s. In summer, men usually wore only a leather breech cloth, and most shaved off at least part of their hair. Women wore leather garments similar to wrap-around skirts. When it got colder, both men and women wore cloaks or shawls over other clothes.

Clothing was often decorated with beads, copper, or paint. Many Indians also decorated their bodies with paint, feathers, and even more unusual items. Colonist John Smith reported, "In each eare commonly they have three great holes, whereat they hange chaines, bracelets, or copper. Some of their men weare in those holes, a smal greene and yellow coloured snake, neare halfe a yard [half a meter] in length, which crawling and lapping her selfe about his necke often times familiarly would kiss his lips. Others wear a dead Rat tied by the tail."

## Hunters and Farmers

The Algonquians relied on their surroundings to survive. All the groups in the Virginia area were expert hunters. They studied the animals carefully to learn how best to hunt them. When they hunted, Native people killed only enough to meet their needs.

Many Native American groups were farmers. Their most important crop was corn, although they planted other foods, such as pumpkins, beans, and melons. The Algonquians planted their crops in small hills, laid out in rows to reduce the number of weeds and make plants stronger. Europeans would not learn the advantage of this style of planting until many years later.

*The manner of their fishing.*

This scene drawn by John White shows Native people in the Virginia region fishing with traps, spears, and nets. The waters in the area provided abundant seafood, including salmon, trout, catfish, oysters, shrimp, and sturgeon.

## Village Life

The Indians usually located their villages near a source of fresh water. Some villages were small; others had several hundred homes. Between six and twenty people lived in each house, mostly members of the same family. Each house had a garden or field for crops. A wall of wooden posts, or a palisade, surrounded most villages to form protection.

Although a woman could become chief of her clan, the position was nearly always held by a man. The jobs of men and women were clearly separated. An English colonist, George Percy, recorded, "I saw Bread made by their women, which doe all their drugerie [everyday tasks]. The men take their pleasure in hunting and their warres, which they are in continually, one Kingdome against another."

Wars did occupy much of their time. Most of the Native groups fought each other over hunting grounds and other resources. Defeated groups were expected to pay **tribute** to the winner.

## The Powhatan

At the time the English came to Virginia, the most powerful Native group in the mid-Atlantic region was the Powhatan. The Powhatan Indians were ruled by Wahunsonacock. His father, a great warrior, had ruled over six groups and united them into the Powhatan **Confederacy**. When Wahunsonacock became

This fortified village was probably the Native settlement of Pomoeiock. It was drawn by the artist John White on his visit to Virginia in 1585.

## The Powhatan Language

Jamestown colonist John Smith recorded some of the language of the Powhatan people. These are a few of the words they used:

| | | | |
|---|---|---|---|
| One | Necut | Nine | Kekatawgh |
| Two | Ningh | Ten | Kaskeke |
| Three | Nuss | Enemies | Marrapough |
| Four | Yowgh | Friends | Netoppew |
| Five | Paranske | Fire | Pokatawer |
| Six | Comotinch | Houses | Yehawkans |
| Seven | Toppawoss | Woman | Crenepo |
| Eight | Nusswash | Man | Nemarough |

chief, he conquered about twenty more groups and took the name Powhatan as a symbol of his power. The Powhatan Confederacy included the Powhatan, the Tappahannock, the Paspahegh, and many other groups, all of which had their own **weroances**, or chiefs.

Chief Powhatan led a confederacy of an estimated two hundred villages inhabited by maybe ten thousand people. When Captain John Smith, a leader of the early settlers, first met Powhatan, he described him with awe. "Arriving at Weramocomoco, their Emperour proudly lying uppon a Bedstead a foote high, upon tenne or twelve Mattes, richly hung with manie Chaynes of great Pearles about his necke, and covered with a great Covering of Rahaughcums [raccoon skins]. At heade sat a woman, at his feete another; on each side . . . were raunged his chiefe men."

At first, the Powhatan people regarded the British settlement at Jamestown as a potential trading partner or as a possible ally in their wars with other Native groups. Soon, however, the two cultures would collide.

**Men and Women**

"The men bestowe their times in fishing, hunting, wars, and such manlike exercises, scorning to be seene in any woman-like exercise, which is the cause that . . . the men [are] often idle. The women and children do the rest of the worke. They make mats, baskets, pots, morters, pound their corne, make their bread, prepare their victuals, plant their corne, gather their corne, beare al kind of burdens, and such like."

*Jamestown colonist*
*John Smith*

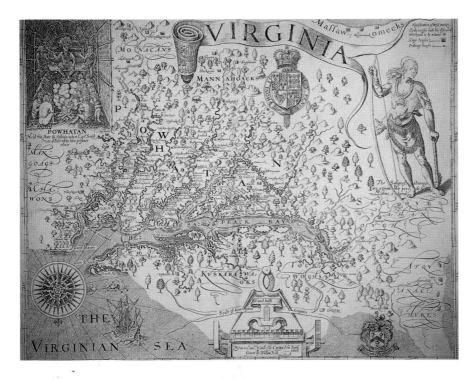

Jamestown colonist John Smith produced this map of Virginia after his return to England. He marked the villages and lands of the Powhatan Confederacy. The land that the English claimed for Jamestown was at the time part of the hunting grounds of the Paspahegh people.

# Chapter 2

# From England to Virginia

## A Royal Charter

By the early 1600s, the English had made several expeditions to North America but had failed to establish a permanent settlement. The English focused on the eastern coast of the continent, north of Florida. This area was not settled by the Spanish, although they, too, laid claim to it. On April 10, 1606, King James I of England signed a **charter** allowing private companies to start colonies in North America. These companies were known as joint stock companies. People who bought shares, or stock, in the companies hoped their investment in an overseas colony would bring them wealth in the form of gold, timber, or agricultural products.

There were other reasons the English wanted to establish settlements. They were eager to acquire land, not least for the growing unemployed population in their overcrowded cities. They also believed that new colonies would offer a good

Like all European kings of the period, King James I believed he had a divine right to rule over his "subjects." He also claimed areas of North America as his own, even though he had never set foot on the continent.

## Roanoke

The first attempt of the British to colonize North America occurred in 1585 on Roanoke Island, now part of North Carolina. However, the colonists didn't have the supplies or the abilities they needed to succeed. Many settlers died. Although England sent new settlers several times, the colony failed to survive. The last group of colonists simply disappeared. No one is sure whether they died or took refuge with local Native people.

market for selling English goods such as woolen cloth. And like other European nations, England had for many years wanted to find a shipping route to the Far East, where other riches lay. (It was thought at the time that there may be a shortcut around the world by going west from a river in Virginia!) Another motive was that of converting Native Americans to Christianity.

## The Virginia Company of London

The king's charter gave the southern half of North America, from what is now Pennsylvania down to South Carolina, to the Virginia Company of London, owned by seven business-men. The charter guaranteed that the colonists and any descendants would have "all liberties . . . as if they had been abiding and borne within this our Realme of England." In other words, they would have the same rights as English citizens.

The charter called for a council in London to rule the colony. But the Virginia Company knew that the day-to-day decisions would have to be made in Virginia. They appointed seven men from among the future colonists to serve on a council that would direct the colony. The names of these men were placed in a sealed box to be opened after the colonists reached Virginia.

By November 1606, the Virginia Company had three ships ready—the *Susan Constant*, the *Godspeed*, and the *Discovery*. But the Company was less effi-cient at recruiting the kind of people who could make the colony a success.

The company seal of the Virginia Company of London carries a portrait of King James I and was used to stamp and seal official documents.

This engraving from 1634 shows Bartholomew Gosnold, captain of the *Godspeed*, on an earlier expedition to North America in 1602. He landed in what is now Massachusetts, where he traded weapons for Indian goods.

## The Future Colonists

The Virginia Company recruited 140 men and 4 boys to sail to North America. Of these, 39 were sailors. The sailors included Christopher Newport, who would captain the *Susan Constant* and be in charge during the voyage; Bartholomew Gosnold, captain of the *Godspeed*; and John Ratcliffe, captain of the *Discovery*.

The other 105 travelers were the future colonists. About half of them were "gentlemen," meaning they came from rich families and were used to having servants or laborers to work for them. Many expected to find gold and then return home to England.

The colonists also included indentured servants. These were poor people who agreed, or were forced, to work seven years without wages in return for their passage to Virginia. After their period of **indenture**, they would be free. Until then, however, they were little more than slaves of the Virginia Company or of anyone who bought their indenture from the Company.

The remaining voyagers included a pastor, a tailor, two surgeons, a blacksmith, two bricklayers, a mason, four carpenters, and a few professional soldiers. Surprisingly, there were no farmers listed among them. Nor was there a mineral expert to take charge of the planned gold mining operations.

## The Colonists Set Sail

The ships were filled with supplies for the journey, livestock, baggage, spare parts for the ships, and parts of an unassembled boat. On December 20, 1606, the three ships sailed out from the port of London. Storms kept them near the English coast for the first six weeks, and many of the men endured terrible sea sickness.

Finally, the winds shifted and they set off across the Atlantic. The ships were crowded and uncomfortable, but the crossing itself was fairly smooth. The travelers stopped at the Canary Islands, the West Indies, and the Virgin Islands. One colonist died on the journey. Finally, after about four months at sea, the ships approached Virginia.

The *Susan Constant* was the biggest of the three ships that took the colonists to Virginia from England. This replica, seen in full sail, is on show at Jamestown Settlement today.

### Great Expectations

"This River which wee have discovered is one of the famousest Rivers that ever was found by any Christian. . . .Wheresoever we landed upon this River, wee saw the goodliest Woods . . . many fruites . . . great plentie of fish of all kindes . . . many great and large Medowes having excellent good pasture for any Cattle. There is also great store of Deere both Red and Fallow. There are Beares, Foxes, Otters, Bevers, Muskats, and wild beasts unknowne."

*Colonist George Percy's first impressions of Virginia*

## Arrival in Virginia

The colonists sighted land on April 26, 1607, two months later than they had expected to arrive. A small party went ashore to look around. George Percy recorded seeing "faire meddowes and goodly tall Trees."

The colonists spent several weeks exploring the area. At last, in mid-May 1607, Captain Newport selected a spot on the newly named James River, some 60 miles (100 kilometers) from the coast. Here, on a **peninsula** now known as Jamestown Island, the settlers would establish James Fort, later called Jamestown.

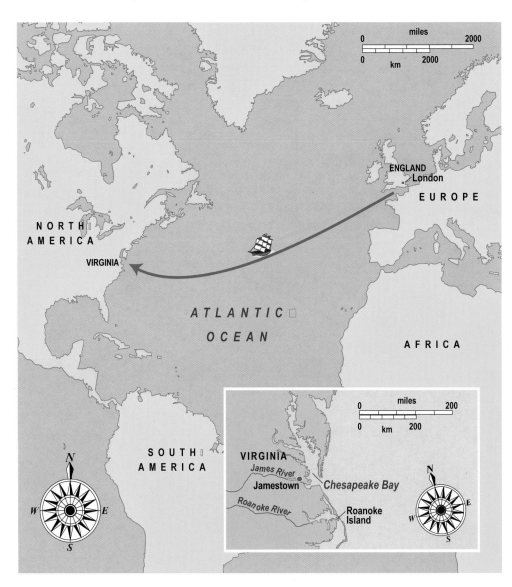

This map shows the route taken by the three ships that sailed to Virginia in 1606. The inset map highlights the Chesapeake Bay area where the colonists chose to settle.

This view of Jamestown Island probably looks much as it did to the settlers arriving in 1607. With its brackish water and population of mosquitoes, the marshland would prove ill suited to settlement.

It was a strange choice, and some argument took place. The colonists' instructions were to find "the strongest, most wholesome and fertile place." Jamestown Island was none of these things. It did not have good drinking water, and the land, half of it **swamp**, was not good for growing crops. It was also plagued with mosquitoes. (It would be two hundred years before it was learned that mosquitoes were not just annoying but carried diseases such as **malaria**.) The site was probably chosen because Hog Island, about 3 miles (5 km) downstream, partly hid the settlement from view. And the **isthmus** connecting Jamestown Island to the mainland was narrow enough to defend from land attacks.

**First Encounter**

"At night, when wee were going abroad, there came the Savages creeping upon all foure . . . with their Bowes in their mouthes. . . . [They] hurt Captaine Gabrill Archer in both his hands, and a sayler in two places of the body. . . . After they had spent their Arrowes, and felt the sharpnesse of our [gun]shot, they retired into the Woods."

*Jamestown colonist George Percy, describing the colonists' first meeting with Native people in 1607*

<br>

# Chapter 3

# The First Months

John Smith was not a "gentleman" like the other members of the colony's council, who thought themselves his social superiors. Smith did not show them the respect they expected.

## The Council

The colonists moved off the ships on May 14, 1607. Before going ashore, the group's leaders opened the sealed box containing the names of the seven men for the colony's council. The three ship captains—Newport, Gosnold, and Ratcliffe—were appointed along with four other men: John Martin, John Kendall, Edward-Maria Wingfield, and John Smith. Captain Newport would serve only until his ship returned to England. The new council then selected Wingfield as its president.

The council immediately faced its first challenge. Relations between Wingfield and Smith were bad. On the voyage from England, only the intervention of Captain Newport had kept the gentlemen from hanging Smith. Now, Wingfield wanted Smith removed from the council. He accused Smith of plotting to have himself made king. Smith insisted on a trial. There was no evidence of a plot, and he was allowed to take his seat on the council.

## First Problems

As supplies were unloaded from the ships, some of them were stolen and sold to Native people. Food supplies were eaten recklessly, with no thought of how or when they might be replaced. President Wingfield instructed some of the colonists to watch for attacks by Indians, others to clear land on which to set up tents, and others to work on building a fort. Some of the men were supposed to dig gardens and others to make fishing nets. But progress was slow. Most of the gentlemen were more interested in searching for gold than building a fort or planting crops.

## Attack on James Fort

At the end of May 1607, Jamestown was attacked by a group of Native Americans. Several of the colonists were wounded and one or two killed. The attackers were probably the Paspaheghs and their allies, since Jamestown was sited on what had previously been Paspahegh territory. The fort at Jamestown was at this point a small and unfinished structure, and it was by no means secure.

Among the many artifacts found at the site of the Jamestown fort were this helmet and breastplate. They were made in the late 1500s and worn as defensive armor during attacks on and by the Native people of Virginia.

The colonists lived in tents when they first arrived. They started to build houses, but their skills were limited.

Historians have pieced together a picture of the original Jamestown fort, based on journals of settlers and archaeological remains. The early structure was a triangle enclosing dwellings and other buildings, but nobody knows exactly how large it was.

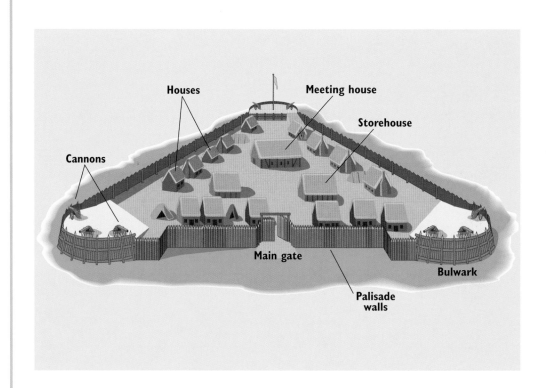

Houses
Meeting house
Storehouse
Cannons
Main gate
Bulwark
Palisade walls

## Friendly Words

"But yet the Savages murmured at our planting in the Countrie, whereupon this Werowance made answere againe very wisely of a Savage, Why should you bee offended with them as long as they hurt you not, nor take any thing away by force. They take but a litle waste ground, which doth you nor any of us any good."

*George Percy recording the words of one friendly tribal chief when members of his group showed resentment at the colonists' presence*

After the attack, the colonists began to strengthen the fort, turning it into a walled, or palisaded, structure surrounding tents and crude huts. Colonist George Percy described it in June 1607 as being "triangle wise, having three **Bulwarkes**, at every corner, like a halfe Moone, and foure or five pieces of **Artillerie** mounted in them."

## Low Supplies

Survival should have been a priority. But instead of planting crops and building houses, colonists were gathering lumber, sassafras root, and ore samples and loading them onto the two ships that would return to England under the command of Captain Newport. The ships sailed on June 22, 1607, leaving behind an uneasy situation. There was disagreement among the colony's leaders, and supplies were dwindling.

## Sickness and Starvation

Within ten days of Captain Newport's departure, the men began to fall sick. After a few weeks, colonists began to die. Some were wounded by Indians, but most were falling prey to disease. Malaria carried by the swampland's mosquitoes and **typhoid fever** and dysentery from the bad water may have been the causes. Year after year, as colonists arrived in Jamestown, they would become sick in the summer months. This period, when colonists either died or developed immunity and survived, was known as the "seasoning."

By the end of summer, there were few food supplies left, and colonists were dying of starvation, too. Smith said later that the small ration of barley each man received contained as many worms as grains. How could they starve when the woods and seas were full of food? Few of the colonists knew how to hunt or fish, and many of the men feared Indian attack if they traveled away from the fort.

When food was running low, President Wingfield was accused of keeping a stock of food and drink for himself and a few friends. Wingfield strongly denied it, but on September 10, 1607, he was thrown out of office and replaced with Captain John Ratcliffe.

### Such Misery

"Our men were destroyed with cruell diseases . . . and some departed suddenly, but for the most part they died of meere famine. There were never Englishmen left in a forreigne Countrey in such miserie as wee were in this new discovered Virginia. . . . Our food was but a small Can of Barlie sod in water, to five men a day, our drinke cold water taken out of the River, which was at a floud verie salt, at a low tide full of slime and filth. . . . Thus we lived for the space of five moneths in this miserable distresse . . ."

*George Percy's account of the first few months in Jamestown*

## Help from an Unexpected Source

By late September 1607, almost half of the colonists had died. John Smith recalled that "the living were scarce able to bury the dead." There were so few of them left and they were so weak that the Powhatans could easily have wiped them out. But instead, the Native people who approached after the harvest that fall carried baskets of food. Percy wrote, "It pleased God . . . to send those people which were our mortall enemies to releeve us with victuals, as Bread, Corne, Fish, and Flesh in great plentie, which was the setting up of our feeble men, otherwise wee had all perished."

It still seemed likely that the colony would fail, especially when President Ratcliffe proved to be no better a leader than Wingfield had been. But Ratcliffe made one good decision: he appointed John Smith as the supply master.

## Smith Takes Charge

Smith stretched his new authority to the limit and put the colonists to work. One of the settlers described Smith's course of action: "[Smith] set some to mow, others to bind thatch, some to build houses, others to thatch them, himselfe alwaies bearing the greatest taske for his own share, so that, in short time, he provided most of them lodgings. . . ."

## John Smith (c. 1579—1631)

Before joining the Virginia Company of London, John Smith had been a soldier. He had fought against a Turkish invasion of eastern Europe, where he claimed to have been taken captive and forced into slavery.

After two years in Jamestown, an injury forced Smith to return to England in 1609. He made another expedition to North America when he explored and mapped the New England coast in 1614. John Smith wrote several books describing his adventures. These were very successful in convincing others to support colonization. Today, Smith's writings are an important source of information about the earliest colonial days. Smith never hesitated to exaggerate to make a good story, however, and he always made sure that his actions appeared noble and heroic. Most historians believe there is some truth in Smith's accounts, but they have doubts about his more colorful tales.

The starving settlers had much to learn from the Powhatans' established agricultural systems. This picture by John White of the Secotan village in Virginia shows their crops, such as pumpkin and corn, at different stages of the growth and harvest cycle.

When that was done, Smith took a small party to trade with the Indians for food. He skillfully won their respect and obtained a boatload of corn. Smith did this on several more occasions, but it was clear the colonists had learned nothing from their experiences. They made no attempt to ration the food. Instead, as Smith later noted with contempt, "what [Smith] carefully provided, the rest carelessly spent."

## Capture

In December 1607, Smith and his men went on an expedition up the Chickahominy River. When their boat got stuck in shallow water, Smith traveled on with two colonists, John Robinson and Thomas Emry, and two Native guides.

Smith and his companions were pursued by the Pamunkey, a group led by Opechancanough, the brother of Powhatan. Robinson and Emry were killed, and Smith was taken captive. After a week or two of being paraded through Indian villages, the prisoner was taken before the great Chief Powhatan at his capital of Werowocomoco.

The chief of the Powhatans as he appeared to John Smith at the time of their first meeting in 1607. This illustration was in Smith's *General History*.

## Pocahontas

In one account, Smith says that he and Powhatan exchanged information, and then he was released and sent home with four guides. In a later account, Smith said there was a feast followed by a long consultation. He wrote that next, ". . . two great stones were brought before Powhatan . . . and thereon laid his [Smith's] head, and being ready with their clubs, to beate out his braines." Smith goes on to say that "Pocahontas the King's dearest daughter . . . got his head in her armes, and laid her owne upon his to save him from death: whereat the Emperour was contented he should live. . . ." Two days later, Powhatan had Smith brought before him. He declared that they would be friends and appointed Smith as a weroance of the Powhatans.

## The Pocahontas Legend

No one knows if the famous life-saving incident ever really happened. It could be that Smith's life wasn't really in danger and the "rescue" was just a ceremony. Others say Smith made up the story after Pocahontas visited London and became famous. Whether it's true or not, Pocahontas was undoubtedly a friend to the English. The colonists would have many occasions to be grateful to her over the next several years.

This engraving of the legendary rescue of John Smith by Pocahontas is based on Smith's own description. There is no way to be sure whether the event ever took place.

# Chapter 4

# Struggle for Survival

## The First Supply

When Smith returned to Jamestown in January 1608, President Ratcliffe and several others accused him of being responsible for the deaths of Robinson and Emry. They intended to hang him, but once again his life was saved, this time by the arrival of Captain Newport.

Newport returned in January of 1608 and was shocked to find that there were only 38 colonists still alive. He brought 100 to 120 new colonists, abundant supplies, and fresh hopes. And he quickly put a stop to President Ratcliffe's attempt to hang Smith. Within a few days of the supplies' arrival, however, disaster struck again. On January 7, a fire swept through the fort, burning buildings and supplies.

This nineteenth-century engraving shows Pocahontas and other Powhatan people bringing food to the struggling settlement at Jamestown. Supplies were sent regularly by Powhatan as personal gifts for John Smith.

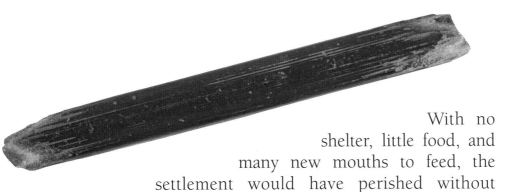

With no shelter, little food, and many new mouths to feed, the settlement would have perished without Powhatan. At least twice a week, Indians arrived with bread, **venison**, and other foods for John Smith.

## Trading with the Indians

In February 1608, Smith and Newport took some men and traveled by river to visit Powhatan. One of the group, Anas Todkill, described their reception: "Powhatan strained himselfe to the uttermost of his greatnes, to entertain us, with great shouts of Joy . . . and the most plenty of victuall [food] hee could provide to feast us." They spent three or four days "feasting, dancing, and trading." Smith wasn't happy with the trading Captain Newport did during his visit to Powhatan. Newport was determined to show how great a man he was by paying far too much for everything. He and his sailors set a bad precedent and destroyed the established trade values for the colonists.

## Gold

Captain Newport had planned to return to England almost immediately, but instead he stayed fourteen weeks, with his crew eating food intended to support the colonists. The sailors stayed because they were determined to take back gold. Two metal refiners had come with Newport, and they led the sailors and colonists into a period of gold fever. One witness said, ". . . the worst mischiefe was our gilded refiners, with their golden promises. . . . There was no talke, no hope, nor worke, but dig gold, wash gold, refine gold, load gold. . . ." Once again, all work for survival was neglected. The returning ships were loaded with the glittering ore mined by the colonists and sailors. When the ore got to London, however, it was found to be worthless **pyrite**.

For Powhatan's "coronation," the Virginia Company sent presents of a crown and mantle, a bed, clothes, and other "costly novelties." Captain Newport, John Smith, and a number of colonists traveled about 100 miles (160 km) to carry out the ceremony. In return, Powhatan gave his old shoes and mantle to Captain Newport.

## A Better Year

From the spring of 1608, John Smith and a new colonist, Matthew Scrivener, supervised the repairs and new buildings in the fort. Smith also spent much of the spring and summer exploring the land and trading with the Indians. When Jamestown held its election for president in September, he was chosen. The Powhatans visited Jamestown frequently, bringing food.

Shortly after Smith's election, Captain Newport returned to Jamestown. He had seventy new colonists, including the colony's first women. The Virginia Company also sent the following orders: find gold, discover a sea route to Asia, or locate the missing colonists from Roanoke Island. Smith was frustrated by these irrelevant tasks when survival was a priority. The Virginia Company's final instruction seemed the most ridiculous: Chief Powhatan was to be crowned. In English tradition this would make Powhatan subject to King James and validate the British claim to North America.

## Change of Leadership

Smith did his best to follow orders, but he also continued to improve the housing and stockpile food for the winter of 1608–1609. That winter stood in great contrast to the previous one. Many of the colonists did not like Smith's strict regimen of work, but it was what the colony needed. The hardship and suffering lessened somewhat, and only a few colonists died.

In 1609, King James issued a new charter, eliminating the colony's council and president. Because of their struggles and problems, the colonists would no longer have any say in who would lead them. A governor would be chosen in London, and he would appoint his own council.

### New Colonists Arrive

The first governor-general was Thomas, Lord De La Warr, an experienced soldier. He sent a lieutenant governor—Sir Thomas Gates—to Virginia with five hundred new colonists. The plan of the Virginia Company was to set up new towns in better locations and use Jamestown just for a port.

For the first time, the new colonists included whole families. After a bad crossing and the loss of the leading ship, the *Sea Venture*, nearly four hundred colonists and sailors arrived in Jamestown. At the time, there were already about two hundred settlers in Jamestown or lodging in neighboring Indian villages, and the colony wasn't prepared to receive several hundred sick and weary travelers. Two **outposts** were established along the James River, and some of the new settlers were sent to both locations.

### The Starving Time

The winter of 1609–1610 was the worst ever for Jamestown. It later became known as the Starving

One of the first advertisements for Virginia was this pamphlet, published by the Virginia Company in 1609. By offering "excellent fruites," it encouraged English people to consider going to North America.

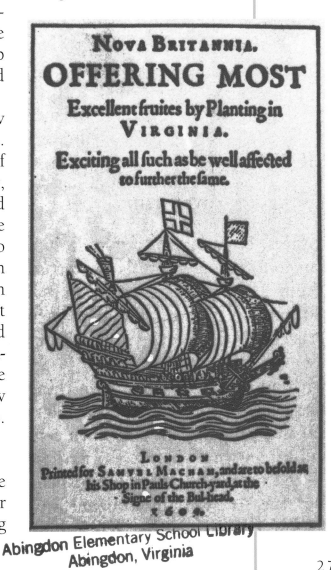

NOVA BRITANNIA.
OFFERING MOST
Excellent fruites by Planting in
VIRGINIA.

Exciting all such as be well affected
to further the same.

LONDON
Printed for SAMVEL MACHAM, and are to be sold at
his Shop in Pauls Church-yard, at the
Signe of the Bul-head.
1609.

In the winter of 1609 to 1610, starvation killed most of the Jamestown settlers. This painting by Sidney King, showing bodies being carried outside the fort's wall to be buried, was one of a series commissioned by the National Park Service. Although painted in the twentieth century, King's works are more accurate than earlier images of Jamestown.

Time. When their stores of grain from the harvest ran out, the settlers had no food supplies. In 1609, a gunpowder accident wounded Smith severely, and he was forced to return to England. Without Smith, the Indian trade had ceased. Supplies were also low among the Powhatan Confederacy because of disruption caused by the white settlers and excessive trade with them. The colonists' pigs on nearby Hog Island had been slaughtered by Indians. Native

## Survival at a Terrible Cost

Colonists became so desperate during the winter of the Starving Time that they ate anything they could to stay alive. First, all of the stock animals, pigs and chickens, were eaten. Then cats, dogs, rats, mice, and snakes. Some chewed leather boots or shoes. They ate snails and even tree bark. Worst of all, some colonists resorted to cannibalism, digging up corpses for food. One man was executed when it was found that he had murdered his wife and planned to stay alive by eating her.

attacks made it nearly impossible to leave the fort to hunt or fish. The colonists remained in their fort, fighting each other over the last scraps of food. They broke apart the houses of those who died and burned the wood to keep warm. Cold, disease, and Indian attack took many of them, but starvation was the main killer. Only sixty people were still alive in the spring.

## Rescue

In May, the colony's new leader, George Percy, decided the few remaining colonists might be able to survive if they moved. He had found that at Fort Algernon, one of the colony's outposts down-stream, the men were thriving.

The move was delayed by the arrival of the people from the lost ship *Sea Venture*, including the lieutenant governor, Thomas Gates. The travelers had built two boats using salvage and trees from the island they had lived on after their ship had wrecked. Expecting to find a thriving colony, they had brought only enough supplies for the voyage. There were now an additional hundred mouths to feed.

The colony's leaders agreed that they could not survive and prepared to abandon the settlement. Gates made sure that he was the last person on board the ships, so that angry colonists could not burn down the now-dilapidated town. On June 7, 1610, they sailed away from Jamestown. The next day, several miles down river, they saw a longboat approaching. Lord De La Warr had arrived at the last moment.

When Lord De La Warr arrived at Jamestown in June 1610, he brought about three hundred healthy new colonists and a year's supply of food and other provisions. Once more, the colony had been saved from extinction.

# New Government

All these tools were found at Jamestown. They are (top to bottom) the head of a brad ax for hewing wood, a funnel (probably once part of a food mill), a file for filing metal, a scuppet (a tool used for digging trenches), and the head of a felling ax for chopping down trees.

The colony in Virginia was faced with several problems. Jamestown had a severe lack of housing for new arrivals, relations with neighboring Indian groups were bad and getting worse, and the colony was still unable to sustain itself.

## The Governors

Lord De La Warr set up a work schedule and required each colonist to do specific tasks. When he returned to England, Sir Thomas Gates was left in charge. His second in command was Sir Thomas Dale, who arrived in 1611 with three hundred soldiers.

Dale set the men to work planting crops, making bricks, and building badly needed houses. He insisted colonists maintain cleanliness and had toilets dug. He also ordered a new well to be dug, since the water from the existing one was as bad as that from the river.

In 1611, it was decided to build a second town, Henrico, 60 miles (100 km) from Jamestown. The colony of Virginia was expanding beyond the immediate Jamestown area.

## Land Grants

In spite of the harsh life, more colonists came to Virginia after 1614 because Dale began offering the settlers land for their own use. Free, male colonists received a lease of 3 acres (1.2 hectares) —2 acres (0.8 ha) to be planted with corn—to farm for themselves. Before this, everything produced belonged to the Virginia Company and went into a common store. Now there was more incentive to work and be productive.

## Dale's Laws

Sir Thomas Dale started enforcing a book of rules that had been written in 1610. The rule book became known throughout the colony as "Dale's Laws." A person who spoke "any disgracefull words" against the colony would have his head and feet tied together every night for a month. Dale refused rations to the sick because he had a "no work no food" policy. There was a long list of crimes that resulted in a whipping and another list that required the death penalty. Two women were whipped for sewing shirts of the wrong length. Colonists who ran away to join Native groups were tracked down and executed, even if they had left because of the lack of decent food. There were many other similar tales.

There was also, at last, the beginnings of an **economy**. Tobacco grown in the Americas had been introduced to England and had become very popular. The type grown by the Powhatans was too bitter for English taste, and colonists for some years had experimented with seeds from the Caribbean. In 1614, a colonist named

As the colony grew and granted small plots of farming land, the settlers moved out beyond the fort. This painting by Sidney King, based on careful research by archaeologists and historians, shows how the settlement probably looked in 1614.

Pocahontas, now renamed Rebecca and converted to Christianity, married John Rolfe in April 1614. In 1616 Pocahontas and Rolfe went to England, where the Virginia Company proudly showed her off. Just before her planned return in 1617, she died of tuberculosis.

John Rolfe produced a successful crop. He sent four barrels of tobacco to England, where it sold well. Within a couple of years, tobacco would be the **cash crop** that the Virginia Company had been hoping for.

## The Peace of Pocahontas

Meanwhile, conflict with neighboring Indians continued and worsened. Since trade had ceased, the settlers continued to plunder Indian cornfields and stores rather grow their own crops. They had also been taking over more and more Powhatan land. The Native people, meanwhile, were housing a number of captives and runaways from the Jamestown settlement, and this too caused conflict.

Chief Powhatan's daughter Pocahontas, who had not been seen since the departure of John Smith, was now in her teens. In 1613, Samuel Argall, a soldier stationed at Jamestown, took Pocahontas hostage. He sent a message to Powhatan demanding corn and the return of men and weapons as a ransom for Pocahontas. Negotiations about her release continued for well over a year.

During this time Pocahontas met John Rolfe, who approached Dale for permission to marry her. Both Dale and Powhatan approved the marriage in 1614. The union brought about a lull in hostilities, and until Powhatan's death in 1618, there was a fragile peace between the colonists and the Native people.

## The House of Burgesses

In 1619, the Virginia Company was reorganized. Several bad harvests had hurt the colony and discouraged settlers. The Company decided that it needed to attract new colonists and encourage those already there. It threw out Dale's Laws and revised and extended the land grant system. Dale's tenant farmers could now become landowners, and new settlers received land of their own.

The Company also set up a new form of government in an effort to keep the support of the colonists. There would still be a governor and council, but there would now be a second **assembly** with the power to make laws. The House of Burgesses would be made up of two representatives from each of the ten districts of Virginia. Each free, adult male could vote for his representative. Women, indentured servants, and slaves could not vote.

This was the first time among Europeans in North America that a group of settlers could decide who would lead them. However, the governor of Virginia, the council, and the Virginia Company in London could overturn any decision the burgesses made.

The House of Burgesses met for several days, once a year, except in an emergency. They were supposed to concern themselves with public welfare and pass the laws required for good government. In practice, however, the burgesses, who were the largest landowners, acted in their own interests. The House of Burgesses also served as the highest **judicial** body in the Virginia colony.

The House of Burgesses met for the first time on July 30, 1619. The burgesses discussed many subjects, including tobacco prices, taxes, and even fines for gambling.

# Life in Virginia

## Changing Population

By 1616, there were four main settlements in Virginia: Jamestown, Henrico, Elizabeth City, and Charles City. There were also several smaller settlements and farms throughout the Chesapeake region. All in all, about 350 people lived there. Of that number, about 65 of them were women and children. Only about 50 people lived in Jamestown.

Over the next few years, Jamestown, although still the capital of the colony, became more of a port of entry and export than a permanently settled community. If anything characterized Jamestown, it was its temporary quality. Neither the people nor buildings lasted long. Over and over again, the settlement was rebuilt after fire, attacks, or neglect. As for the people, they died in large numbers from illnesses they brought with them or contracted soon after their arrival. Between 1607 and 1624, more than 6,000 of the total 7,300 immigrants died.

The Virginia colony spread out along the James River and farther afield. Small settlements called "hundreds" and the larger plantations became districts within the colony. They had their own members in the House of Burgesses.

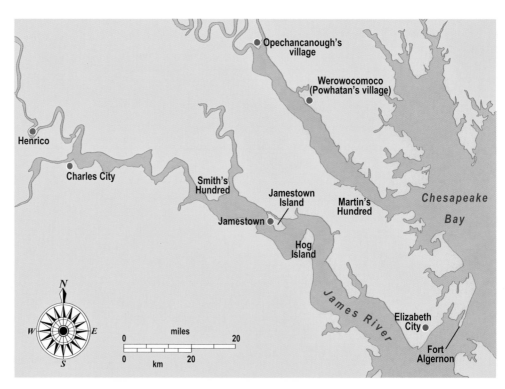

Of those who lived, most left the town for the more wholesome and productive region around it. Jamestown Island itself was really only suitable for raising pigs and grazing cattle. The rest of the colony was busy producing tobacco.

## The Tobacco Boom

After John Rolfe's successful export, the colonists saw the possibility of wealth in growing tobacco. Virginia rapidly became a one-crop region after 1616, when Thomas Dale left and restrictions on the growing of tobacco were lifted. Instead of growing food to feed themselves, the colonists were gripped by tobacco fever.

In 1618, only two years later, 50,000 pounds (23,000 kilograms) of tobacco were exported from Jamestown to England. Life soon became centered on the crop. It even became the currency of the colony.

Barrels of tobacco are loaded onto ships in the James River. In 1628, more than 500,000 pounds (230,000 kg) of tobacco were shipped from Jamestown to Europe.

## The Bride Ships

The population of Jamestown always remained overwhelmingly male. But as the Virginia colony expanded into the surrounding region, the Virginia Company recognized that the settlement needed women in order to survive. In 1619, hoping to make the colonists more contented and committed, the Company sent ships to Virginia carrying ninety women. Another hundred arrived in 1620 and fifty more in 1621. Not surprisingly, the richer men in the colony usually secured the brides; the women were priced at a minimum of 120 pounds (55 kg) of tobacco.

### Living and Dying in Servitude

Growing tobacco required a large amount of labor. And the cheapest labor available was that of indentured servants. The colonists, some of them freed recently from their own Company indentures, simply had to pay the passage across the Atlantic for these individuals and provide them with a little food, some clothes, and a roof over their heads. In return, they got seven years of work from them.

Most indentured servants were kept in appalling, unhealthy conditions. They were supposed to receive supplies, such as tools and seeds, when their term was up, but they usually died before completing their years of service. By 1660, about fifteen hundred indentured servants were arriving in Virginia every year. In some years, more than half of them died within twelve months.

> **A Loathsome Custom**
>
> "[Smoking is] a custome lothsome to the eye, hatefull to the Nose, harmefull to the braine, daungerous to the Lungs, and in the blacke stinking fume thereof, neerest to resembling the horrible Stigian smoke of the pit that is bottomelesse."
>
> *King James I of England*

Opechancanough, seen here rallying his warriors against the white settlers, had been a powerful leader in the Powhatan Confederacy even when his brother was still chief. Opechancanough was nearly ninety years old in 1644 when he was finally captured and killed by colonists.

### End of the Peace

Conflict between the white settlers and the Native inhabitants of Virginia was a fact of daily life, and once more there was open warfare. As the colonists took more and more land for tobacco farming, the Powhatan people were losing their homes and their cornfields. When Chief Powhatan died in 1618, his brother, Opechancanough, took leadership of the confederacy. Opechancanough watched as the English settlements grew and demanded more concessions

The attack of 1622, as envisaged by the Flemish engraver Theodor De Bry ten years later.

from his people. He knew that if he didn't force the English out, the Powhatans would eventually be forced out themselves.

Opechancanough planned carefully, and in March 1622, he attacked. He and his warriors took the English completely by surprise. The Powhatans killed or captured about 350 out of the colony's population of 1,400, and they completely destroyed Henrico. Attacks continued from both sides over the next years, including Opechancanough's last major assault in 1644. But the white colony grew steadily, and by 1700, there were only about 1,000 Powhatan people left.

A report on the attack of 1622 and conflict among directors in London led to the fall of the Virginia Company. On May 24, 1624, King James **revoked** the Virginia Company's charter, and Virginia became a royal colony under the control of the Crown.

## Populations in the Colony and the Town

The population of Virginia began to grow rapidly. In 1634, there were 5,000 white people living in the colony, and by 1642, there were 15,000. By the mid-1600s, there were hundreds of farms in Virginia connected by roads to the main settlements.

The population of Jamestown did not grow at a comparable rate. In fact, it often declined. In 1625, it had 125 inhabitants; in 1667 there were 160 residents; and in 1676 only 96 people lived there. Over the years, several attempts were made to build a more permanent town with a larger population, but they all failed.

The residents of the towns were mostly officials, soldiers, and servants. There were also skilled laborers, including blacksmiths and carpenters. There were a few craftspeople, such as glass makers and tailors. But their profits never matched those to be made in tobacco, and crafts never flourished in Jamestown. Most goods such as furniture were imported from England.

## The Planter Society

The majority of settlers lived outside the towns. They were mostly farmers and planters, increasingly with wives and children, and an ever-growing servant population. Illness and death continued to undermine family life, but a **plantation** society was developing in Virginia.

The colony's leaders sought to reproduce English society, and they did so by recreating a system in which land, wealth, and power belonged to the privileged few. But there were some differences.

In England, people's place in society was determined by their birth. In Virginia it was difficult, but not impossible, to climb the social scale. In theory, any free person, even a woman, could own land. In its first session, the House of Burgesses urged the Virginia Company to grant land to wives "because that in a newe plantation it is not knowen whether man or woman be the most necessary."

Prospective brides arrive in Jamestown from England. Although they were advertised as "young maidens," many of them were convicts who had been shipped overseas instead of being sent to prison.

## The Beginnings of Slavery in Virginia

In August 1619, a Dutch ship docked in Jamestown and sold the colonists 20 Africans as "bound servants." In the early days of Virginia, slavery did not take hold because the system of indentured servitude already existed. But in the late 1600s, the flow of servants from England decreased, and planters began to import African slaves.

At first, some of the Africans brought to the colony were treated as indentured servants, and some even gained their freedom. In 1670, however, a Virginia law declared that "all servants not being Christian," and brought in by sea, were slaves. The slave population there grew from 3,000 in 1681 to 260,00 by 1782.

This picture from a tobacco label of the early 1700s shows a wealthy plantation owner overseeing his slaves.

The headright system was introduced in 1619 and gave 50 acres (20 ha) of land to a head of household for every person he brought to Virginia. This made it easy for those with enough money for slaves or indentures to then acquire huge areas of land.

This meant that the power and wealth eventually shifted from the small population of "gentlemen," who had no wish to stay in Virginia forever. Instead, through the ruthless acquisition of Indian land and the labor of many servants and slaves, a new ruling class of permanent colonists emerged.

# Bacon's Rebellion

In spite of treaties between the colony's governors and the Native people, white settlers in Virginia took more and more land from the Indians. Here, a group of settlers attack a Native settlement in 1675.

## Sir William Berkeley

The royal governors sent from England rarely stayed in Virginia for long, until the arrival of William Berkeley in 1642. He governed Virginia until 1652 and then again from 1660 to 1677.

In his first term, Berkeley achieved many **reforms** and improvements. His popularity waned in his second term when he showed preference for the concerns of the wealthy few rather than those of ordinary citizens and smaller farmers and planters. Taxes were high, tobacco prices were low, and it was hard for any but the richest landowners to make a living.

At this time, plantation owners in the outlying areas of Virginia were pushing ever farther

## The Commonwealth

Sir William Berkeley's rule as Governor had an eight-year gap. Civil war in England led to the establishment of a **commonwealth** under Oliver Cromwell. Virginia and Governor Berkeley remained fiercely loyal to the Crown and declared the new government "traitorous." The English government then passed the Navigation Act of 1650 that said only English ships should carry goods back and forth from English colonies. Virginians were dependent on their trade with the Dutch and defied the order. Cromwell then sent a military force to Virginia in 1652. Berkeley surrendered, and the House of Burgesses took over governing the colony. Berkeley was reelected as governor in March 1660, a few months before the restoration of the **monarchy** in England.

into Indian lands. Governor Berkeley had trade agreements with the Native people and was trying to maintain peace with them, but the settlers on the frontier wanted more protection from the Indians whose lands they were taking.

## Bacon's Rebellion

One of the outlying settlers was Nathaniel Bacon, who wanted to fight Indians to secure his land. He raised huge popular support. Bacon was joined by some leading Jamestown "gentlemen," most notably Richard Lawrence and William Drummond, who resented the newly wealthy planters and merchants. In June 1676, Bacon and Lawrence marched into Jamestown with five hundred men. Bacon demanded a commission to attack the Native people. At the same time, the General Assembly—made up of the governor's council and the House of Burgesses—passed twenty acts of reform. These were known as "Bacon's Laws," although they were probably written by Lawrence and Drummond.

Soon after, Berkeley declared Bacon a traitor. Tension increased until the governor fled Jamestown for his safety. On September 19, 1676, Bacon and his men entered the town. To prevent the governor and his council from returning and resuming government, Bacon, Lawrence, and Drummond burned down Jamestown. Things were at a standoff when Bacon suddenly died from illness on October 18, 1676. Without a leader, support for the rebellion declined, and the uprising crumbled.

Nathaniel Bacon confronts Governor William Berkeley in Jamestown, demanding changes in the government of Virginia. The two were cousins by marriage, and Berkeley had recently appointed Bacon to the council.

41

# Conclusion

### The Decline of Jamestown

Jamestown never quite recovered from Bacon's Rebellion. Some of the houses were rebuilt, and the House of Burgesses continued to meet there until 1698, when a fire destroyed the statehouse. The colony leaders decided to move the capital to Williamsburg, and Jamestown was abandoned. The island was part of two local plantations, and then just one, in the following two hundred years.

### Recovering Jamestown

Since the late nineteenth century, archaeologists have been working to uncover the remains of Jamestown. In 1901, the Association for the Preservation of Virginia Antiquities started excavating the site of the Jamestown church.

Historians have been given many clues about the original settlement from these archaeological explorations. For years, it was believed that the land on which the original fort once stood had been washed out to sea, but then archaeologists discovered part of the fort's foundation. They have since uncovered more than 250 feet (76 m) of the wall, a bulwark, and three cellars. They have also found more than 350,000 artifacts from the earliest days at

Remnants of the original Jamestown fort are still being found. This pit, uncovered in one of the bulwarks, was possibly where soldiers stored the gunpowder for their muskets and artillery.

Jamestown, including a pit filled with discarded armor and weapons.

## Visiting Jamestown

Every year, thousands of visitors flock to Jamestown. They come to see the excavation site of the original Jamestown and remains of the old town, including the restored 1639 church, the graveyard, and the foundation of the statehouse that was destroyed by fire.

At Jamestown Settlement, a reconstructed Powhatan village has demonstrations of grinding corn, weaving ropes, and making dugout canoes. The recreated fort shows the settlement as it may have been in about 1610. Visitors can climb aboard replicas of ships, the *Susan Constant*, the *Godspeed*, and the *Discovery*.

The Powhatan Indian village at Jamestown Settlement offers demonstrations of Native American crafts, such as the tanning of deer hides seen here.

## The Legacy of Jamestown

Jamestown was the first permanent English colony in North America. As such, it was, in effect, the birthplace of the United States of America. The original settlers made many mistakes and suffered terrible hardships as a result. Jamestown never succeeded as a community, and for most of its inhabitants from 1607 to 1698, life was unimaginably wretched. However, the House of Burgesses was the first legislative assembly in the English colonies. Started by the Virginia Company for its own purposes, the assembly was used to further the interests of the privileged, but it evolved into something more important. Similar legislative assemblies soon appeared in all the royal colonies. Eventually, they broadened their bases to represent more fairly the interests of all people. After independence, legislative assemblies continued to be an important part of government in the United States. And today, state legislatures are vital to the lawmaking process.

# Time Line

1606 ■ April 10: King James I of England grants the Virginia Company of London the right to start a colony in North America.
December 20: Three ships, *Susan Constant*, *Godspeed*, and *Discovery*, set sail from London.

1607 ■ May 14: Colonists disembark at Jamestown Island.
Settlement of Jamestown is established.
December: According to legend, Pocahontas saves John Smith's life.

1608 ■ September: Smith elected president of Virginia colony.
October: First female colonists arrive in Jamestown.

1609 ■ King James I appoints governor in England for Virginia colony.
October: John Smith returns to England.
"Starving Time" begins.

1610 ■ June: Governor Lord De La Warr arrives as colonists prepare to abandon Jamestown.

1611 ■ Sir Thomas Dale arrives.
Settlement of Henrico is founded.
Dale's Laws begin to be enforced.

1613 ■ Pocahontas is taken hostage.

1614 ■ John Smith explores and maps New England coast.
Pocahontas marries John Rolfe.
First shipment of tobacco sent to England from Jamestown.

1617 ■ Pocahontas dies.

1618 ■ Powhatan dies and Opechancanough assumes leadership of Powhatan Confederacy.

1619 ■ Reorganization of Virginia Company results in establishment of House of Burgesses and headright system of land grants.
First Africans are brought to Jamestown.

1622 ■ March: Powhatan Indians capture or kill about 350 colonists.

1624 ■ King James I revokes charter of Virginia Company and makes Virginia a royal colony.

1642 ■ Sir William Berkeley takes up position as royal governor of Virginia.

1676 ■ June: Bacon's Rebellion begins.
October 18: Nathaniel Bacon dies.

1698 ■ October: Statehouse in Jamestown burns down.

1699 ■ Capital of Virginia moves to Williamsburg.

# Glossary

**Algonquian:** any of the Native peoples of North America who spoke one of several Algonquian languages.

**artillerie:** now spelled *artillery*. Large, heavy guns such as cannons.

**assembly:** group of people gathered together for making laws or decisions.

**bulwarke:** now spelled *bulwark*. Wall or other structure that acts as a defense against attack.

**burgess:** person who has a citizen's rights in a particular borough. In early Virginia, this meant male, white landowners and came to mean those who represented their borough in the legislative assembly.

**cash crop:** crop, such as tobacco or coffee, grown mainly to sell rather than to provide food for the farmer.

**charter:** official grant of privileges by a governing body to an individual or group.

**colony:** settlement, area, or country owned or controlled by another nation.

**commonwealth:** nation, state, or government in which authority belongs to the citizens rather than to a monarch.

**confederacy:** alliance of groups that agree to act together and support each other.

**democracy:** government system in which people vote on decisions or elect representatives to vote for them.

**economy:** system of producing and distributing goods and services.

**indenture:** contract between employer and worker in which the worker agrees to work for a set period of time.

**isthmus:** strip of land connecting two larger areas—for instance, a peninsula to the mainland.

**judicial:** having to do with the justice system and administering of laws.

**legislature:** group of officials (usually elected) that makes laws.

**malaria:** feverish illness caused by a parasite carried by mosquitoes.

**monarchy:** nation under the rule of a king or queen rather than the rule of an elected government.

**outpost:** outlying settlement, such as the smaller settlements around Jamestown or a military post on the frontier.

**peninsula:** piece of land jutting out into water but connected to the mainland on one side.

**plantation:** large farm where cash crops are grown and large numbers of laborers or slaves are employed.

**pyrite:** shiny, yellowish mineral sometimes mistaken for gold.

**reform:** change in society intended to improve conditions.

**revoke:** cancel or take back.

**swamp:** very wet land partly covered by water.

**tribute:** payment by a group or nation to a ruling nation, person, or protector.

**typhoid fever:** serious, infectious disease that makes people very sick and feverish.

**venison:** meat from wild game, especially from deer.

**Virginia:** region of North America first named by English in 1584. Its boundary to the west was not defined, but the original area stretched farther north and south along the coast than the present state of Virginia.

**weroance:** chief of a Native group or tribe.

# Further Information

## Books

Doherty, Kieran. *To Conquer Is to Live: The Life of Captain John Smith of Jamestown.* Twenty-First Century Books, 2001.

Hermes, Patricia. *The Starving Time: Elizabeth's Diary, Book Two, Jamestown, Virginia, 1609.* Scholastic, 2001.

Sakurai, Gail. *The Jamestown Colony.* Children's Press, 1997.

Sewall, Marcia. *James Towne: Struggle for Survival.* Atheneum Books for Young Readers, 2001.

Sita, Lisa. *Indians of the Northeast: Traditions, History, Legends, and Life.* Gareth Stevens, 2000.

## Web Sites

**www.apva.org** Pictures from the Association for the Preservation of Virginia Antiquities of archaeological explorations and artifacts found at Jamestown.

**www.historyisfun.org** Information about Jamestown Settlement from the Jamestown-Yorktown Foundation.

**www.vcdh.virginia.edu/jamestown** The University of Virginia's Virtual Jamestown project.

## Useful Addresses

**Jamestown Settlement**
Jamestown-Yorktown Foundation
P. O. Box 1607
Williamsburg, VA 23187
Telephone: 1-888-593-4682

# Index

Page numbers in *italics* indicate maps and diagrams. Page numbers in **bold** indicate other illustrations.